Here is a simple collection of prayers to use at home or in school through the year. The illustrations help to relate the prayers to particular seasons and events.

© LADYBIRD BOOKS LTD MCMLXXIX

Book of Prayers

Compiled and illustrated
by DAVID PALMER

Ladybird Books Loughborough

January

Thank you, Father, for another new year which brings many new things. New people to meet, new lessons to learn, new places to visit and things to see.

Have you seen the patterns that frost can make on a window pane or on plants and fences outside? Try looking at them through a magnifying glass.

5

January

Heavenly Father, we know that
the winter can be cold and cruel
with the trees bare, the ground
hard and the ponds frozen over
with ice. Please help us to
remember to feed the birds
who visit our homes and parks.

When snow makes everything white we may enjoy it, but it is hard on the creatures who cannot find enough food to live on. You can put out scraps during the day for the birds, or hang some fat or nuts up, and watch them enjoy their feast.

February

Thank you for our homes and families, dear God. It can be nice and cosy at home during the cold weather. We have warm clothes, hot meals, and comfortable beds to sleep in.

We are lucky to have warm homes. Many people, because they are old or poor, have little food or warmth and may not be able to go out. Try to help those who have difficulty in caring for themselves in the winter.

February

We pray for those, dear Father, who have to work in bad weather out of doors. They bring us fish from the waters around us, oil and gas from the sea bed below and look after animals and crops on the land.

You will probably have noticed the first flowers coming up now. Look for the white snowdrop and the purple, yellow and white crocuses, and think of those who cannot enjoy these pleasures.

March

The spring flowers and blossoms cheer up our countryside and gardens after the dullness of winter. We thank You, dear God, for giving us these bright colours to enjoy.

The wild flowers you are most likely to see now are the yellow primroses and mauve violets on banks by the roadside and in the woods. In towns, the green tips of bulbs can be seen, breaking through the soil.

March

Thank you, Father, for the birds.
Many are coming back to our
country now that the weather is
getting warmer, and are looking
for somewhere to build their
nests where they can look after
their young.

You may find a bird's nest in a hedge or tree or even in your shed or garage. Try not to disturb it until the young have flown. Find out where the migrant birds have come from, and wonder at their ability to survive such long journeys.

April

Thank you, Father, for the new life that Jesus showed us when He came back to life on Easter Day. We see new life around us at this time of year, with lambs being born in the fields, and new leaves on the trees and hedges.

The jelly-like spawn the frogs, toads and newts lay in the ponds, is hatching into tadpoles. You could collect some in a tank with some water-weed for them to feed on and when they have developed into adults, return them safely to the pond again.

April

It is not always sunny at this time of year. We can have rather miserable, rainy days when we cannot do things outdoors. Thank you, Father, for museums and other interesting places to visit at these times.

We can learn a lot, from museums, about the people who lived many years ago, and about the world around us. Many museums have libraries where particular interests can be studied further.

May

We thank You, Father, that with the coming good weather we can enjoy fairs and other outdoor events. Please help us to keep these customs where we meet and enjoy the company of others.

At this time of year there are lots of fairs, parades and other interesting customs that have been going on for hundreds of years. Look for teams of Morris dancers in towns and villages during the summer.

May

We thank You, God, for all the
blossom and flowers at this time
of year. Thank you for our sense
of smell and sight. Help us to
help those who are blind or
cannot go out.

Every flower has a purpose. It may be the food source for many insects. Try not to damage living things, because others like to enjoy them too, and the wildlife of our country depends on our respecting it.

June

We pray for all the peoples of the world. Please, God, let us understand each other better, so that we can share our ways of life and not dislike some people because they are different.

There are many different religions and beliefs around the world. You could find out about some of them and see how, when and why they started.

June

We thank You, God, for the long hot days and warm evenings. In the country we can listen to the skylarks high above the fields during the day, and in the town the blackbirds singing till dark.

In the warm summer evenings you can smell the scent of flowers like the honeysuckle and rose. Look out for the night-flying moths that are attracted to them.

July

When it is sunny and warm we can spend the day seeing interesting things with our families and friends. Thank you, Father, for these opportunities of sharing our enjoyment.

There are many safari parks, zoos and nature reserves to visit. Try to find out some facts about the animals you are likely to see, before you go.

July

Please, Father, help us to remember the things we have seen and learnt during the past months. Thank you for the friends we have at school. We might not see them for a while when we break for holidays, so help us to make the most of our work and play together.

At this time of year many butterflies are about. Swallows and swifts swoop low after flying insects, and in the fields you will probably hear the grasshoppers and crickets before you see them.

August

We thank You, Father, for our holidays. We can enjoy the seaside in the fine weather, playing in the sea and on the sand. We can explore the rocks and pools and look for some of the fascinating creatures You have created.

When the tide goes out, many crabs and small fish
are left in rock pools. If you are careful you can
watch them without disturbing them. On the
shore-line you may see wading birds feeding on
the creatures in the sand.

August

We thank You, Father, for the opportunities of travel. Many people are now able to visit faraway places by air, road, rail or sea. Please help us to learn from travelling and to understand Your world a little more.

Motorways can be long and tiring, but look out for the kestrel hovering over the roadside on the lookout for mice and voles.

September

At this time of the year we may
be starting a new school or
class, with new friends and
teachers. We ask You, dear God,
to be with us, and to help us in
our learning.

You may be able to keep certain animals as pets at school, where they can be cared for and studied. Lizards and other small reptiles can be kept, as well as mice and guinea pigs.

September

Thank you, Father, for all the gifts You give us at harvest time. From the seeds and grain planted in the soil, You bring us fruit and vegetables, and wheat for our bread.

Around the end of September, most churches have their Harvest Thanksgiving Service. The inside of the church is decorated with many kinds of produce from the land. See if you can recognise the different types of food displayed in your local church.

October

Thank you for the changing seasons, dear God, and the pleasure they give us. At autumn time we can see the leaves turn to red, brown and gold.

The leaves fall and form a rustling carpet under the trees, then they gradually decay into the soil, adding goodness to it which helps to support the life of the tree they came from. Mushrooms and other fungi can be seen growing up from under the fallen leaves.

October

We can see the animals busy at Autumn time, gathering winter supplies of food and nest materials. Thank you, Father, for such interesting creatures that give us so much pleasure.

Squirrels can be seen in the Autumn, busily collecting nuts for their store. The fieldfare, a large type of thrush, feeds on the ripening berries of hawthorn and other bushes.

November

We pray for city life, dear God.
Cities are busy, interesting
places with buildings and parks,
entertainments and history, but
they can be very lonely places
for some people.

Think of people who live alone in cities. They often have no friends and find a busy city very lonely. Perhaps there are lonely people in your own town or village who need friendship or help.

45

November

These chilly days have their beauty in Nature. Thank you, Father, for the misty scenes of spiders' webs sparkling with moisture in the frosted hedges.

Trees may seem lifeless in winter, but we have the chance to see the wonderful pattern of their branches and the different shapes they make.

December

Thank you, dear God, for the passing year. We look forward to the future with interest. As we grow older we learn more about our own world and the other worlds in Your universe.

Many astronauts have now walked on the Moon and robot exploration craft have made missions to planets, like Mars, to see if any forms of life exist there. Think of the vast spaces in our wonderful universe.

December

Thank you, Father, for
Christmas. We spend many
weeks preparing for this festival
of giving, and remember the
special gift You gave us of
Jesus.

The tree we use at Christmas was named by an eighth-century English missionary, St Boniface. In Germany he chopped down an oak tree that was being used in a pagan service, and there, trying to grow among its roots, was a small fir. He dedicated it to Jesus as the Christ tree, the evergreen symbol of Peace.